One day a rabbit in a pink dress ran across the grass. It ran up to Jelly.

"Help me, help me," it said to Jelly.

"Help me to get out of this dress. I do not like it."

Jelly looked at the dress.

It had lots of pink frills.

It had six glass buttons at the back.

Jelly pulled a button. Pop went the glass button. Pop, pop, pop, pop, pop went all the glass buttons.

But the rabbit was still stuck in the pink dress. Hop, hop, hop went the rabbit. It got very cross.

"Help me, Jelly," it said.

So Jelly held the pink dress down on the grass and the rabbit got out of it.

"Thank you," said the rabbit.

"I am sorry for the fuss."

The rabbit ran off across the grass.

Then Jelly got into the pink dress.

Look at silly Jelly in a frilly dress.